MW01096326

The Art of Growing Through Feedback

A Practical Guide on How to Give and Receive Feedback Graciously

By Adrian Pei

Text copyright © 2016 Adrian S Pei
All rights reserved

While all stories in this booklet are true, some names and identifying information have been changed to protect the privacy of the individuals involved. All images used under license from Shutterstock.com and Stockvault.net.

Table of Contents

Introduction

The best leaders relentlessly pursue feedback, even when it's hard to hear or uncomfortable to give. That's because they know it's vital to personal, professional, and spiritual growth. They know healthy feedback is an essential part of thriving relationships, partnerships and organizations. Put another way:

Feedback is how we maximize the wisdom of the people in our lives to reach our full potential as leaders.

But how do we handle feedback? After all, many of us never grew up in households where feedback was a normal part of communication or interaction. So we never cultivated the habit of asking for input, and learning how to receive criticism graciously. It's no wonder so many of our experiences with feedback are awkward, intense, or de-motivating. And when we have negative associations with feedback, why would we want more of it?

Fortunately, it doesn't have to be this way! Learning to navigate the waters of feedback is an art that we can grow in, with practical skills we can learn. There are phrases we can learn to say. There are questions we can learn to ask. There are principles we can learn to apply. And the more we practice these things, the more we become comfortable with feedback! Soon, the process can become normal, comfortable, and believe it or not — even fun.

The following booklet is a collection of articles I've written that are a compilation of lessons I've learned from my past decade of working in leadership development and human resources. I've given my fair share of feedback to a variety of people in different contexts, and I've received even more feedback on my own leadership. I wanted to share the mistakes I've made and situations I would handle differently now that I've learned and grown more.

This booklet contains ideas on making feedback creative and fun, how to give and receive feedback effectively, and about how feedback relates to topics like power and ethnicity. I've tried to write the chapters in a conversational tone with plenty of personal stories and sample scripts of things we can say in dialogue. I also list some books and resources that have helped me learn about feedback, if you care to research the topic in more depth. At the end of each chapter, I include some questions you can use if you're using this booklet for discussion in a small group or a coaching relationship.

I hope you enjoy this booklet and please do give me any input and feedback (adrianpei@gmail.com), as I'd love to hear and learn from you!

Thank you,

Adrian Pei

Chapter 1: How To Make Feedback Fun (Really!)

There are simple, practical things we can do to make feedback more helpful and enjoyable for us, and for other people.

Okay, let's face it. Although giving and receiving feedback are incredibly important in leadership, too often the process ends up being awkward or intense. We sometimes walk away feeling defensive, de-motivated, or confused. And we're not exactly sure what went wrong. This can make us want to just avoid it in the future. However, I'm trying to create a different "feedback culture" in my relationships and life!

How can this be done? Maybe it doesn't have to be that complicated. I want to walk through a number of real-life examples I've encountered where feedback hasn't been done that well, and where it has been done well. Sometimes I've been on the receiving end on feedback, and other times I've been on the giving end and have had to learn from my mistakes.

To start with, I'm going to cover four core principles (in this booklet) that I've come to believe about feedback. The first is this, Feedback Principle # 1:

We need to ask for feedback more regularly.

Feedback can mean a lot of things to different people, but at its heart I try to see feedback as an opportunity to grow — whether we're growing ourselves, or helping others to grow. In my experience, the best leaders relentlessly pursue feedback and growth.

And so behind it all, I'm learning to operate under the mindset that feedback is a good thing, *even when it's not delivered in the best way.* No matter what motivates a person to give me feedback, there's usually a kernel of truth behind what they're expressing that I can take to learn and grow as a leader. So I try to take the attitude of:

"With every piece of feedback I get, I have the opportunity and privilege to grow. I get to become a healthier person, and a more effective leader!" This helps make me grateful for feedback.

Of course, it can be deflating and discouraging when feedback is delivered poorly, and we'll discuss this more in future chapters. But here's one way to think about that: when feedback is done poorly, that's an opportunity for *me* to give feedback in a healthy way to the person who delivered it. In other words, give feedback about the feedback, to the givers of the feedback. Try saying that five times quickly. What I mean is that we have an opportunity to model good feedback, even when it's done poorly to us.

In light of the importance of feedback, we need to ask for feedback *much* more regularly and consistently in our lives and leadership. I've found feedback turns out way worse when it's only rarely given, and that's when it becomes awkward and intense. People tend to over-think it, get much more amped up or defensive, and so on. It just feels like so much is on the line.

So this is how I'm trying to work it out in my life and household. I'm trying to ask for feedback for small things throughout the week that aren't always super intense. Like, "how did I do arranging the pillows on the couch?" :) But seriously, things like:

"Did you think I was a little too strict with the kids tonight, or a little too lenient?"

"Would it have helped if I had given you a few more minutes of help today with cooking, or did I do enough?"

I'm trying to get into a **regular rhythm** of doing this, so I get more used to it, and my family gets more used to it as well!

Or at work, you could ask your boss or colleague:

"Do you think my presentation was a little too long or a little too short? Any simple ideas to tweak it to be better?"

"Are there small things I could do to communicate better or more efficiently with you?"

I did this recently as I was working on a project. I asked my collaborator a few days into the project, "Is the amount I'm communicating with you too much, or not enough? Or do you prefer for us to just figure it out as we go along?"

Sometimes I also ask, "Is e-mail working out, or is it easier for you to interact by phone?" If we ask these questions early in the process, it can really help set some clarity.

But the point is that if we establish a culture of asking for feedback regularly, it actually gives permission to *both* sides to speak up and make helpful adjustments along the way. It communicates, "I'm okay if you tell me something I could do differently, or if there are changes that would be helpful." And usually when the other person feels they can do that, they tend to follow suit and give you permission to do the same for them. Win-win situation!

Here are a few things I've learned about these kinds of statements listed above:

1. When we take the initiative to ask for feedback ourselves, it reduces defensiveness. If *we* ask for feedback rather than wait for someone to give it to us, we're much more likely to take it better.

2. It helps to give options when we ask for feedback.

When we're too generic about our request ("What did you think of the chicken I cooked?") it can be harder for people to know what to say and how.

Instead, it helps to be specific and give options ("Was the chicken a little too salty, or not quite salted enough?"). In my experience, this is more likely to get us helpful feedback that's not too overwhelming, intense or confusing.

3. Again, ask for feedback often.

We can start by trying for once or twice a week, and then slowly increase until we get to once a day.

4. Make it casual sometimes.

Let's mix up our requests for feedback. Ask for both small and big things, both casual and more serious.

Try it tonight, and let me know how it goes. Seriously! I want to hear how it works for you, as I continue to try it myself. Remember, the best leaders relentlessly pursue feedback and growth.

Questions for Small Groups & Coaches:

- What's your first reaction when you hear the word "feedback?" Did you grow up learning how to give & receive feedback well? Explain.

- Think of a time that someone handled feedback or criticism well. What did you appreciate about what they did?

- How regularly do you ask for feedback in your life and leadership?

- *Action Step:* Write down two simple, casual "feedback" questions you can ask of two trusted people in your life. Follow through this week.

Chapter 2: How to Decide If and When to Give Feedback

Three crucial questions to ask ourselves before we start giving feedback.

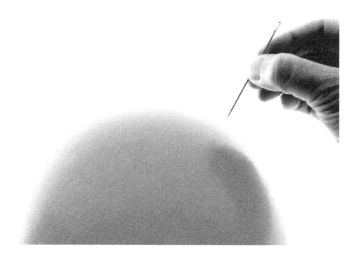

In the last chapter, I wrote about the principle that "we need to ask for feedback more regularly."

However, ASKING FOR feedback and DELIVERING IT are two vastly different experiences! Sometimes we are tempted to jump in and give feedback out of emotion or reaction to something. If we are to deliver feedback consistently, we need to learn how to do it with thoughtfulness and sensitivity.

In light of that, here's Feedback Principle # 2:

We need to discern if and when it's appropriate to give feedback, before we give it.

For instance, one night my wife was showing me notes for a presentation she was about to give at an event. I skimmed the notes and immediately said, "This is good, but I think it's too much content and it gets a bit confusing. I think you can take a lot of unnecessary stuff out, and rearrange things to be more organized."

Well, my wife didn't take my feedback too well and felt pretty deflated. Sure, I could say "I was only trying to help and had the best intentions." I could even blame her for "not being able to take constructive criticism."

OR, I could eat some humble pie and reflect on what I did that wasn't helpful, and what I can do better next time!

So let's break it down into three crucial questions that can spare us some unnecessary pain:

1. **Is it worth it to give feedback? (Rank on a scale from 1 to 10)**

Was it worth it to give my wife feedback? Overall her presentation was very good, and would have gone well.

Sure, there were a few things that could have been better, but that's the case for most presentations.

Sometimes we have to discern and pick our "battles," depending on how high the stakes are.

When we're considering whether or not to give constructive feedback, one practical idea is to rank the importance on a scale from 1 to 10 in our own minds, and seek to prioritize the items that rank highest in number. There are some things we really should devote our energy to giving feedback on, like when somebody close to us has hurt us with something they did, and it's jeopardizing the relationship. Or if my wife's presentation was in front of thousands of people and had huge implications for her job status, and her notes were horrific.

Then there are some items that aren't necessarily worth the feedback, like when I'm looking at a friend's essay that's 95% great. In a situation like that, I'd rather take the time to offer encouragement and blessing to the 95% rather than isolate and criticize the 5%. Or if my wife has spent all day running errands to help our family and she messes up the last errand by picking up the wrong item for dinner...

maybe it's better to thank her for everything she did, rather than critiquing her for getting one thing wrong.

We need to look at the full picture and prioritize what's worth speaking into, and what's not.

2. Am I the best person to give feedback?

Here's one eye-opening fact about my wife's presentation: she didn't *ask me* to give her feedback. It would have been one thing if she had said, "Adrian, I'm working on a presentation and think it could be better. Could you please take a look and give me some constructive feedback?" But she didn't! She simply showed me her notes, and I took it upon *myself* to give her feedback! I assumed I was a good person to give her feedback, and that it was my role to do so. Maybe all she wanted was to share what she was working on with me, and that's why she felt so deflated when I turned the experience into a critical workshop.

We need to ask ourselves, why are we the best ones to give feedback? I've seen many evaluations after events, and the people asked to give feedback just don't have enough context. They might not be the right people to give feedback. If we sense that we don't have the full picture or won't necessarily have the best judgment, we can always direct people to other sources that will.

Here's another question I've found helpful to consider: *Why are we motivated to give feedback about something, or to someone?*

Many times I've found that we can use the medium of negative feedback to channel our frustrations about other unmet needs or unexpressed emotions. For instance, we're so unhappy with our boss that we unload our criticism through the "feedback survey" he or she sends out about a conference.

Before we give feedback, we should ask ourselves if there's something else we need to express or resolve with the person in question. If so, it probably calls for a different kind of conversation. We must be careful not to veil our unresolved concerns or struggles as "giving feedback."

3. When is the right time to give feedback?

Maybe I could have given my wife helpful feedback on her presentation, if I had chosen better timing. Maybe I could have simply acknowledged all the work she had done that evening, which is probably what she really needed, and asked the following day if she needed any further help.

Maybe if I had affirmed her efforts, she would have actually asked me for feedback. There are a lot of ways to do this!

In closing, **the main takeaway is that we should think first, before jumping right into giving feedback.** Yes, we shouldn't be afraid to deliver regular and consistent feedback, but we must do it with care. Asking these three simple questions will help us discern if and when feedback is appropriate.

If feedback is appropriate, we then need the courage and skill to move forward and deliver it well. We'll cover how to do this in the next chapter.

Questions for Small Groups & Coaches:

- When you have "put your foot in your mouth" and given feedback when you probably shouldn't have? Explain. If you could do it over, how would you do it now?

- Which of the three categories above are hardest for you to judge: (1) how important it is to give feedback about an issue, (2) whether you're the right person to deliver feedback, or (3) when is the right timing to give feedback?

- What's your "feedback style?" (see the Appendix) Explain and discuss.

- *Action Step:* Write down a list of 3 things you wish could have been handled differently this week by people in your life (e.g. Your best friend flaked on a get-together, your spouse forgot to take out the trash, your child threw a tantrum, a coworker made an inappropriate joke about you). Rank their importance to you on a scale of 1-10. Along with your group or coach, think through whether it's worth giving feedback about any of the situations. If a situation is a "2" or a "3", consider letting it go. If you have a "9" or a "10" on your list, try following through on giving feedback this week.

Chapter 3: Feedback: The First and Most Important Thing to Say

One simple thing you can say to eliminate 90% of problems when you're delivering feedback.

In the last chapter, we discussed how to discern if and when to give feedback. Now we'll cover Feedback Principle # 3:

When feedback is appropriate, we need to learn to deliver it well, not avoid it because we're afraid of doing it badly.

Delivering feedback well requires two things: courage and skill. We need to be brave enough to give feedback when it's necessary or important, and we need the skill set to do it thoughtfully and effectively.

I've found that most problems arise when we have one without the other. Sometimes we charge into giving feedback when we're fired up about something or someone, and don't really take the time or thought to learn how to do it sensitively. *In other words, we have courage but lack skill.* Often we're tempted to defend this by saying "we have good intentions." But good intentions aren't enough… after we've told our friend that she has a weight problem, does it really make her feel better when we say, "I was just trying to help?"

However, I think the majority of the time we avoid giving feedback at all, because we don't want to mess things up. Regardless of whether we have skill, *we lack courage.* And this is why so many important conversations never happen, whether it's employees addressing a communication breakdown with a coworker or their boss, or family members getting to the root of why a fight happened.
On which side of the spectrum do you land?

Do you tend to have courage, but need to grow in skill? Or do not give enough feedback or have enough hard conversations, because you're afraid of doing it poorly, or of what it might do to your relationships?

The good news is that either way, *there's something you can do about this!* We'll cover some practical things you can do to deliver feedback with skill, and I'll recommend some books and resources as well. Let me start with something extremely simple that you can say that could save you a lot of grief, before you attempt to deliver your next piece of feedback.

Try saying this:

"I really want to say this in a respectful way, but I'm still learning how to give feedback well. I apologize for the parts that don't come out well, and could you please tell me afterwards what I can improve for next time?"

How does reading that feel to you? Liberating or empowering, hopefully?

Here are a few things this accomplishes:

- **It communicates a desire to respect and value someone.**

  This sounds incredibly simple, but it's amazing how often this element is not part of a feedback conversation.

- **It acknowledges that our words and feedback have an impact on this person... and we *care* about that impact.**

  Again, so simple but incredibly important.

- **It communicates that we're a work in progress as we learn to give feedback well, and we're inviting them to be part of that process!**

  In other words...

  Yes, we're asking for their feedback... about our feedback! It can set the tone for the entire conversation, from defensiveness to openness.

  Again, when we give permission to others to help us through their feedback, they are more likely to open themselves to us as well.

  Addressing the 3 things listed above can go a long way... in my opinion, it can eliminate 90% of the problems we tend to encounter during feedback conversations. It's not only more honoring of people... it's more effective too!

  It's something you can apply right away, in just 2 sentences... so try it and see how it works for you!

Questions for Small Groups & Coaches:

- Which do you need and want to grow in more: the courage to engage feedback more often, or the skill to handle it well?
- What's one small but helpful piece of constructive feedback you've gotten over the past few years? Explain.

- *Action Step:* Write down a situation that's bothering you, that you could give feedback about. Role-play the conversation with your group or coach, and try starting off the conversation using the paragraph written above. Get feedback on how you did, and then follow through on giving the actual feedback this week.

Chapter 4: How to Deliver Feedback Effectively

Breaking down effective feedback: 7 practical steps that can be executed in less than 1 minute.

Okay, we've said the first and most important thing to start a feedback conversation. Now what? First of all, here are some technical details:

Deliver the feedback in person if at all possible. If not possible, use a video call... but avoid e-mail at all costs.

Deliver the feedback directly with a person, one-on-one. In general, don't do it in a group setting or through another person. Don't say, "My friend told me she thought you were acting a little strange at dinner." Speak for yourself, and let your friend speak for him or herself.

Now that we're ready to have the actual conversation, here are the most important things I'm learning to do, along with some examples of what we might say. Let me start by writing out one example that should help illustrate:

"Bill, thanks for making the time to talk. You are one of our most skilled and gifted leaders, and you've invested many valuable hours into creating this volunteer service program. I truly believe your program can have a huge impact on the community, and so I wanted to share some constructive feedback in the hopes of helping it to succeed. First of all though, I want you to know how much I love the clear way you organized the program, and the thoughtfulness behind the interactive exercises. My biggest concern is the length and some of the wording which I fear may be a little overwhelming for participants.

I hope my feedback came across in the right way. What are you hearing me say?"

I wrote out this example, because I wanted to illustrate that a feedback conversation doesn't have to be incredibly long or complicated. The paragraph above only takes about 35 seconds to say (you can time it), and then goes straight into interaction with the person. Don't be deterred by thinking it will take you forever to do!

But each of the elements in the paragraph are intentional and important, so let's break them down one-by-one:

- #1: Affirm & Acknowledge: This must come first.

Affirm the Person: As we start giving feedback, first affirm the relationship and explain *why* it matters to us. Don't just say, "I value you." Say: "I value you as a colleague who's been a valuable contributor to our team and company" or "You are an important person in my life, and our friendship has helped me to grow a lot as a person."

Acknowledge the Journey: Next, acknowledge the effort or journey of the person. "You've worked many hours, and poured your heart and soul into this project. It must not have been an easy process." Or: "We've been through a lot together, and you've persisted through the ups and downs."

- #2: Explain our Heart and Purpose.

Communicate the heart behind **why** you want to give feedback. "I really believe in this project, and want it (and you) to succeed, but I feel it can be even better. That's why I wanted to give you some feedback." Or: "I want our relationship to be even closer, but I've been sensing some resistance in my interactions with you, and I wanted to talk about it in hopes that we can resolve anything that needs resolving."

- #3: List the Positive.

Share some of the good things first. "Don't get me wrong, there are a lot of great things I see in your project. Here are 3 specific things I love, and why."

- #4: Address the Main Issue or Concern Concisely.

Now share the most important concern or issue you're wanting to give feedback on, or work through. Try to keep it to 1 or at most 2 things, and keep it concise. More than that tends to be overwhelming and confusing for people.

- #5: Interact about the Main Issue.

Ask Them to Summarize: "I hope that came across in the right way. *What are you hearing me say?*" Give them space to share how they would paraphrase your feedback to them. This is one of the most important steps! It will help you understand how they are taking in and interpreting what you said.

Clarify (if necessary) and Engage: If you feel they didn't hear you in the way you intended, feel free to clarify or try again. And then engage with them about the topic — back and forth — as needed. It may be helpful to offer resources and constructive possibilities, if we can do that without making it seem we know better or are trying to "take over."

- #6: Affirm the relationship, and thank them for their time.

- #7: Follow Up.

Don't leave this one out! I have neglected to do it, and have paid the price for it. No more than 1-2 days after your feedback conversation, e-mail or call the person and say, *"Thanks again for hearing my feedback, I appreciate your willingness to engage it. How are you doing since our conversation?"* Quick and simple: a two sentence e-mail will do the trick.

So these are the elements of a feedback conversation that have been most effective for me.

Again, it may feel like a lot of steps, but remember the paragraph above which took 35 seconds to say. What's required in a feedback conversation will vary, depending on the maturity of the person we're talking to, and our relationship and history with them. But all things being equal, I have experienced the most consistent success when I've included all the elements listed above.

The good news: as we practice, it will take less time and feel more and more natural to deliver feedback. And the neat thing is that we won't feel like we have to build up as much courage to do it. But again:

We won't get comfortable with feedback unless we make it a more consistent and regular part of our lives and relationships.

The only way this happens is to do it. Start off by practicing it with the people you feel most comfortable with. Respond to opportunities when you're asked for feedback or input... I just had a chance to "practice giving feedback" last week! These opportunities come up fairly often when we're looking out for them.

Practice, and practice often! I've learned more by having three 5-minute feedback conversations with my wife, than by trying to memorize books or seminars. Though if you are interested in a book, check out *How to Have That Difficult Conversation*[1] by Dr. Henry Cloud and Dr. John Townsend which has greatly influenced my principles and approach.

In the next chapter we'll cover the art of how to receive feedback well.

Questions for Small Groups & Coaches:

[1] Dr. Henry Cloud & Dr. John Townsend, *How to Have that Difficult Conversation* (Zondervan, 2015)

- Who's one of the best people you know at delivering feedback graciously? What do they do well, and why do you think it works?

- At this point, what do you think you most need to work on related to learning how to deliver feedback graciously? Share with your group or coach.

- *Action Step:* Write down a situation that's bothering you, and role-play with your group or coach a feedback conversation you might have, using the 7 steps listed above. Get feedback on how you did, and follow through on the actual feedback conversation this week.

Chapter 5: Putting Negative Feedback into Perspective

Which is worse: criticism or indifference?

We've discussed some of the art of delivering feedback well, but now we turn our attention to the other half of the equation — how do we receive feedback? How should we respond to criticism?

This brings us to Feedback Principle #4:

> **We need to learn to receive feedback well, and grow from it without losing ourselves in the process.**

I learned this lesson after **writing a blog on a popular website about ethnicity, gender, and sexuality**[2]. It was a unique time when the media was filled with news about NBA player Jeremy Lin, and there was unprecedented interest in what Asian American leaders had to say. Well, the first comment that came in was extremely critical to say the least. To paraphrase loosely, it basically told me to "suck it up and stop complaining."

I'll be honest that the words stung, and largely because I had written something that was personal and meaningful to me. I felt a lot of emotions, from anger (*Who is this guy, and what does he know, anyway?*) to doubt (*Wait a minute... maybe I shared too much or could have written things in a better way*). I felt the temptation to go into self-protective mode, and defend myself whether through a response or through no response at all.

---

[2]   http://nextgenerasianchurch.com/2012/02/09/jeremy-lin-asian-american-male-sexuality/

We all are prone to these kinds of feelings or thoughts when we hear negative feedback, especially when it's not delivered in a respectful way. But through that experience and others since, I'm learning to view negative feedback in a different light.

Here are a few things I'm learning:

- **Indifference can be worse than negative feedback.**

I know this may sound crazy, but even criticism is a way that someone is trying to connect with us. Even if it's delivered in an awful and invalidating way, criticism means that someone has noticed you or something you've done, and has made an effort to respond.

Not everybody goes that far. In fact, if you're in the business of writing or putting yourself out in front of other people, you know that the vast majority of people do not even see you or think about you (or what you've done) at all. It's not necessarily because they don't like you, or because what you did wasn't valuable. There's just too much out there to keep track of it all!

It's kind of like this:

1. Most people don't read or notice.
2. Out of the few that do, most of those skim.
3. It's the tiny minority that take the time to respond or write in.

So in this day and age, if people write in, they probably have been moved in some way by you, or what you've done. And that's usually a good thing!

- **Negative feedback doesn't necessarily mean we've failed.**
Of course, negative feedback often means we need to reevaluate and see where we need to improve or grow. However, there are certain times when a negative response is actually a sign that we've succeeded, not failed. For instance, there are times when we need to confront destructive behavior in people, or even challenge the "way things have always been done" with hard questions. At times when we do these things effectively, it's normal to expect a negative response. People don't like being

confronted, and there's usually resistance from the status quo when it's challenged.

As a writer and creator, I am going to be involved in projects that challenge people to rethink or re-evaluate things. *If I do that successfully, shouldn't I expect there to be some who disagree and dislike those ideas?* Even if I write with tact and clarity, this can (and will) happen. But that's what I want... I'd rather create something meaningful that goes deep into peoples' minds and souls, rather than write a hundred articles that are risk-free, but never scratch the surface of people's hearts.

I recently stumbled upon an interview with mixed martial artist Ronda Rousey, and something she said stuck with me:

> "I don't need crowd approval, I need crowd passion... [Mixed martial arts] is an art. And art isn't supposed to be nice, it's not supposed to be liked. It's supposed to make you feel something. So I don't want to specifically make crowds cheer or boo. I just want to make them feel."[3]

---

[3] https://www.youtube.com/watch?v=V0L6kO2ij-A

Sometimes we can assume that success means that people like us, but that's not always true. We do want to improve our leadership and work to not offend people out of insensitivity or carelessness, but sometimes even when we do things well there can be negative responses or reactions. And that's okay.

- **Negative feedback isn't always about us — even if it's sparked by us.**

Not everything is about us, and we have to remember to not take everything personally. Sometimes when someone reacts negatively to something we've done, it's because they are wrestling through something else that's unresolved in their minds and hearts. As someone who believes in God, I acknowledge that he may be doing something in peoples' lives that's bigger than just whether or not they like me.

As I work on projects that are meaningful to me, what I'm learning is to accept the journey that people are on, as they react honestly to something I've done. Humans are emotional beings — and their feelings and reactions are important, even if they don't seem to make sense at first.

When I wrote the article I mentioned above, one of the other bloggers on the site told me, "I love real talk, even if it includes strong emotions or offensive language sometimes. Raw is okay if it's honest, because that's real."

I love that. I'd rather hear where people are at — in all the messy parts of their journey and process — than hear something that makes me feel better, but is manufactured or fake.

- **Don't forget "we signed up for this." Each of us.**

If we want to grow and to lead well, there's simply no way to do that without putting ourselves out in front of other people. And as we've seen, that inevitably will expose us to negative feedback. Yes, we can try to avoid people and hide, but that will also lead to consequences that will eventually come back to us. There's really no escaping the reality that we will have to face negative feedback. It's part of the deal of life and leadership. The only question is, will we face it so we can learn and grow from it?

I frequently read sports articles, which are filled with criticism and second-guessing of nearly every decision of the leaders. After every lost game or season, a thousand blaming fingers point in every direction.

The most successful players, coaches, and executives respond not by dodging, but by facing the criticism head-on. Last year, I remember reading about a college football offensive coordinator who was asked, "Do you think there's something about your job that makes fans feel more justified in criticizing?" He responded: "The quarterback gets it, head coach gets it, offensive coordinator... they're going to get it. It's part of the deal, and that's what we signed up for."[4]

We are all in the "feedback business." That's part of the deal of life and leadership. The good news: if we learn to face it, we can take big steps of growth as leaders! And it all starts with putting negative feedback in perspective.

In the next chapter, we'll cover some specific steps that will help us receive feedback more graciously.

---

[4] http://www.theolympian.com/sports/college/pac-12/university-of-washington/huskies-insider-blog/article41706228.html

Questions for Small Groups & Coaches:

- Describe a time that you received criticism that you felt was extremely harsh or off-base. What were the circumstances? How did you feel and react?

- What was off-base and wrong about the criticism? What might have been the "kernel of truth" behind it?
- *Action Step:* What do you think is one of the biggest areas you need to grow in your leadership right now? Share with your group or coach, and then share this with a trusted person in your life this week. Ask them to encourage you, and check in with you about this issue regularly.

Chapter 6: How to Receive Feedback Graciously

A recipe for how to make someone's blood boil.
And how to cool it down in 3 simple steps.

I'll never forget the most ridiculous customer service experience in my life. I had arrived home to celebrate my wife's birthday, only to discover that the bakery had given me the wrong kind of cake. I called the store, and they told me the manager would call me back… but I heard nothing for two days. When I finally called again and got the manager on the line, she was rude and in complete denial.

Me: "I asked for the red cake, but I got a yellow cake."

Manager: "Well, that's not possible, because our staff know the difference between a red and yellow cake."

Me: "I don't know what to tell you. They gave me a yellow cake."

Manager: "Um, I don't know what to tell you either. Nobody in our store would have done that."

Me: "Are you saying it's not possible that your staff made a mistake?"

Manager: "No, I'm not saying that."

Me: "Are you saying I'm making this up or that I made a mistake?"

Manager: "No."

In retrospect, this conversation is even a little comical. I mean, if her staff can't make mistakes and neither did I, what exactly did she think happened? The cake changed colors while I was driving home? I said the word "red" but her staff worker heard the word "yellow"?

But on a more serious note, I was getting pretty frustrated at this manager's complete unwillingness to take any responsibility. No hint of an apology or anything. After a couple more exchanges, I eventually asked her:

"Do you want to make money? Why would I as a paying customer want to come back, when my order was messed up and there's no acknowledgment of a mistake? Why wouldn't I tell my friends about this experience and this phone call, and tell them not to come to your store?"

She couldn't hear it. She hung up the phone.

Clearly this was NOT a good way to receive feedback. The thing is, there were so many other ways this manager could have handled that phone call.

She could have said, "Mistakes do happen" or "We don't want any of our customers to leave unsatisfied" without having to admit that she or her staff were necessarily the ones in the wrong.

She could have said, "I'm sorry to hear that... Is there anything I can do to make this right?" She wouldn't necessarily have to give me a refund (and I wasn't even asking for one)!

Instead, she violated almost every single value we've been discussing in this feedback booklet. There was no acknowledgment of my reality or the impact on me, no desire to respect me as a customer, and so on.

Needless to say, I've never been back to that bakery since and I've told many of my family and friends not to go there. Learning to receive feedback well isn't just a matter of improving one's "EQ" skills.

Our ability to receive feedback well impacts how successful and fruitful we are in our work and relationships.

In contrast, I'll never forget when a hotel manager responded as well as possible to a problem I had. She came to visit my room in person, asked to hear what happened, took responsibility, offered to make things right, and then followed through. She even sent a plate of fruit to my room as a gesture. I'll always remember that, *even more than the hotel room or amenities themselves.*

Think about that for a second! I might not have even remembered this hotel much beyond a general negative impression. But simply because she knew how to receive feedback, this manager transformed a bad experience into a positive association that stands out in my memory! And you better believe I'll be giving that hotel repeat business for years to come.

Good and bad leadership have *tangible, measurable, and lasting* consequences.

So as we think about how to receive feedback well, here are 3 steps to consider:

Step One: Thank the other person for the feedback.

Say, "Thank you for caring enough to talk to me about this. I know it might have been easier to avoid me or just not say anything at all."

Step Two: Clarify the feedback.

Paraphrase what you think they're saying. Say, "What I'm hearing you say is..." "Would you say that captures it well, or would you want to clarify anything?"

Be a Detective, not a Debater: During this step, I've learned that it's important for us to seek to understand why we're getting this feedback, much like a detective would. It's more effective than getting into a logical debate about details. People nearly always have a reason for what they're saying, even if it doesn't appear rational.

Feedback: "You're late again. This is getting frustrating."

Bad Response: "I'm only ten minutes late! And the last two times, it was only five minutes."

Better Response: "I'm sorry to keep you waiting, especially since this isn't the first time you asked me to come earlier. Do you feel that I'm not respecting your time, or is it something else? I want to understand and hear where you're coming from."

The primary goal during this step is to make sure the other person feels heard. Make sure that happens before you push back, justify, or give counterexamples. The other person will simply not hear you, if you try doing that.

It's hard to listen well when someone is listing grievances and getting emotional... but hang in there, because it's well worth it!

And keep in mind that "hearing another person" does not necessarily mean agreeing with them, or losing your own opinions or voice in the conversation. You are simply validating that they have had an experience that is real *to them*. We'll talk more about this in our next post.

Step Three: Ask permission to share.

Say, "Thanks again for your feedback, I'll take a look at that in the weeks to come. May I also share some of my thoughts that may provide some context?"

Some people might think receiving feedback well is just about "taking it in the gut" and not saying a word. While there certainly are times when it's better to just listen and not respond, I actually lean away from this approach. I think it's healthy to be able to hear other peoples' thoughts and views, and still be able to speak our own minds respectfully. The goal is that both people are honored, and neither is invalidated. But that means we don't minimize ourselves or our own voices either!

In the next chapter, we'll discuss more on this topic of how we can speak up for ourselves, while remaining gracious in the feedback process.

<u>Questions for Small Groups & Coaches:</u>

- Describe a time that you received criticism that you felt was extremely harsh or off-base. It could be the same situation you discussed last week, or a new one.

  Play the role of "detective" and try to figure out two good reasons why that person delivered the criticism to you.

  - Role-play the situation, trying to handle it according to the three steps listed in this chapter. Ask your coach or someone in your group to play the role of the person giving you the harsh feedback. After the role-play, get feedback on how you did.

  - *Action Step:* If your group or coach feels it is appropriate, send an e-mail to the person who gave you that feedback, explaining how you've thought more about the situation and you now understand more about why they said what they did. If appropriate, set up a meeting to discuss in greater depth, so you can practice what you've learned about listening well, and also sharing your own thoughts at the end.

Chapter 7: Disagreement ≠ Defensiveness

Allow yourself to be influenced by others, but believe in what you stand for.

If you've ever seen the cooking competition TV show "Chopped" (or any reality competition show), it's almost the ultimate sin to talk back to a judge. I've seen cooks try to justify why they made a decision about the flavor or presentation of their dish, and the judges nearly always just shake their heads. *Don't make excuses. Stop being defensive. Know your place... you're talking back to an Iron Chef!* Those seem to be the unspoken messages to the cooks.

As a result, most competitors tend to stay silent. They simply hear the judges' critiques, nod their heads in understanding, and say "Thank you."

When it comes to receiving feedback, I sometimes feel a similar sense of hesitation or even paralysis after someone has given me some criticism. Should I just be silent and "take it," even when I have a thoughtful response, or even if there's clearly much context the person is missing? But if I speak up with any of my own thoughts, will they simply think I can't take constructive criticism, and that I haven't truly heard them?

It's a tough thing to figure out.

Here's the principle I try to operate by:

Allow yourself to be influenced by others, but believe in what you stand for.

Sometimes I hear celebrities or athletes say, "I don't care what other people think. I don't ever listen to criticism, because people don't know what they're talking about." While this may be true some of the time, I've found that the best leaders don't shut themselves off completely from feedback.

They're able to listen with an open mind, while not losing confidence in their identity and values as they do that.

So let's say we're receiving some constructive feedback. How can we apply this principle of allowing ourselves to be influenced, while still maintaining our own voice and opinions? Here are 3 different approaches we can try. In each case, we should always make sure the other person feels *fully heard* before we talk!

1. Listen first, then ask permission to share.

Like I wrote in the previous post, we can offer our own perspective after we listen. It is okay to ask a couple of clarifying questions (e.g. "When you said my talk is hard to relate to, do you mean it needs more personal examples, or would something else be more helpful?"). Just don't use "leading" questions to make your own point. ("So do you think I could have possibly had the time to do everything you suggested for this project?") :)

After you've heard the person well, ask permission to share your own perspective:

"Thanks again for the feedback and I'll take a closer look at what you're saying. May I also share some of my thoughts that may provide some context?"

2. Broaden the person's perspective.

Another approach is to say something like: "I really appreciate hearing your thoughts. I've actually been polling a lot of different people, and some have agreed with what you've said, while others have said the opposite. So I have to look at the entire picture of feedback and then judge how to proceed based on what seems best."

Sometimes this can help a person see that not everybody has the same experience they do.

3. Give them feedback on their feedback.

Most of the time I don't elect to do this… I only save it for times when a person has been particularly harsh in their criticism. When that's the case I might say:

"Thank you for caring enough to give me this feedback, and I'll learn from it. I do have to confess that hearing it was a little hard for me, given how challenging this project has been.

Next time, it would really help me if you could start by listing a few positive things before diving right into the flaws. That would help me know that not everything I did was off-course. Did that make sense... what are you hearing me say to you?"

Fair's fair. If someone is going to dish out harsh feedback to you, it's not too much to ask them to receive some feedback as well — especially if we deliver it graciously. Maturity doesn't mean being a doormat. There are times when people simply won't "get it" unless we speak up and let them know how their words or actions have impacted us. We can speak up as long as we do it respectfully.

But wait... there's more! Sometimes we can say things to help "guide" others before they give us feedback. This applies when we're asking for feedback from others, or entering a situation where we know feedback will likely be offered.

For instance:

"Please be gentle, because this project is a labor of love and I've already been through 3 rounds of feedback and revisions. However, I do still want to hear your honest thoughts. Can you just list the good along with the bad as you give feedback?"

A lot of people may not know how we're feeling, or what kind of process or journey we've been through, so we have to guide them to help them understand what we need. I've found when I do this, it really helps others, and I have some of the most constructive feedback sessions.

Overall, remember Feedback Principle # 4:

We need to learn to receive feedback well, and grow from it without losing ourselves in the process.

Allow yourself to be influenced by others, but believe in what you stand for. Or as Rudyard Kipling writes in his famous poem "If": *"Trust yourself when all men doubt you, but make allowance for their doubting too."*

In the end, it's a matter of stewardship. Why is feedback valuable in the first place? As we talked about from the beginning, it's an indispensable tool for our own learning and growth as leaders. Yes, we will get all varieties of opinions from people with different backgrounds and limited perspectives, and only we have the full picture of all these pieces of feedback. We have to be the ones to see the kernels of truth in these pieces, to judge which parts need to be contextualized or translated, and then to make the necessary changes and applications in our lives.

But we can only do this if we view feedback as helpful pieces to build us up, rather than break us down. We can treat feedback like sharp arrows that we try to dodge and yank out when they stick in our skin. Or we can treat it like segments of a larger mosaic or painting that give us incredible insight we would have missed, without all the various sources of feedback!

In exploring all these techniques and details, let's not forget the bigger reason why feedback matters.

Questions for Small Groups & Coaches:

- Who in your personal life, or in the public eye handles criticism well? Describe what you think they do well.

- Ask a friend or coworker: "What's one small thing I could do to improve our communication or relationship?"

- *Action Step:* Write down an item (personal or work-related) that you'd like to get feedback about. Before you ask for feedback, write down 1-2 sentences that will help prepare the other person/people to best give you feedback (like in the chapter above). Share this with your group or coach, and get some feedback on it. Role-play if it's helpful.

Chapter 8: Feedback and Power

Feedback is a tool of power, and it can create environments of freedom or oppression.

This year, the Golden State Warriors set the all-time record for most wins in a regular NBA season... in the year after they won a championship! It's becoming clear that they've got something special going, not just in terms of basketball success but in the culture of motivated leaders they are creating.

One story that illustrates this perfectly tells of how last year during the NBA Finals, coach Steve

Kerr made a major adjustment in strategy upon the suggestion of a video coordinator.

A New York Times article describes how Nick U'Ren was watching old video footage and thought that playing the smaller but athletic Andre Iguodala instead of center Andrew Bogut might be a good move.

Kerr listened, agreed, and went with this feedback... and it may have turned the tide in the series, as the Iguodala was able to defend LeBron James fairly well. After the Warriors won the championship, Kerr publically gave credit to U'Ren for the idea. **The article** describes how Warriors player Shaun Livingston reacted to this decision:

"I've played for nine different organizations, and I've never seen anything like that. This wasn't even an assistant coach; it was a video coordinator. And Steve Kerr listened to him, and he did it. All the bridges are open here. There's an open forum of ideas. A good idea really can come from anywhere. And that kind of thinking has to start at the top."[5]

---

[5] http://www.nytimes.com/2016/04/03/magazine/what-happened-when-venture-capitalists-took-over-the-golden-state-warriors.html?_r=1

Wouldn't you want to work for an organization or a team like this?

None of this is accidental, of course. Kerr didn't have to listen to U'Ren's thoughts or feedback. Or he could have claimed credit for the strategy. But he didn't, and think about how empowered and motivated that must have made a "lowly" video coordinator feel. *See how players like Livingston took notice of Kerr's actions, and the impression it made on him.* People see the decisions of leaders, and how and why they make them. This creates a leadership culture. Kerr has used his power to create a culture of freedom and empowerment.

In contrast, I've seen countless organizations, families, and teams where an oppressive environment has taken over. Almost invariably, these are places where feedback is rarely (if ever) requested or desired. Questions like, "How do we need to change and grow?" and "Who do we need to listen to more?" are simply not asked. When a team member offers critique or feedback, he or she is met with defensiveness and resistance by the leader... and the "voiceless group" of the other team members who don't speak up for themselves.

After a few experiences like this, the person feels like they're just being a pain for always bringing up "problems" or "negativity," and they feel discouraged. They start to think, "Maybe I really am the problem here." Soon they stop offering feedback or opinions at all, because what difference will it really make? And they now too have become part of the voiceless group. Power has been used to protect and preserve control.

I've experienced it, and I've seen it happen over and over again.

A number of years ago, I heard a female television producer talk about a famous movie director who started off with a few brilliant films. To get this done while he was still relatively unknown, this director had to collaborate and seek a lot of input and feedback along the way. That's just what you have to do when you're starting out. However, once this man found enough success that he could "call his own shots," he stopped asking for feedback. It became all about him and his brilliant vision.

Because this director no longer had to listen or submit to people who could refine his work, or keep him in touch with reality, he got lost in his own world. As a result, his next few films were unsuccessful and he's now faded into obscurity.

The television producer shared her observation that the most successful directors continue to solicit feedback and invite correction, even after they have risen to the top in Hollywood. They use their power to create an environment where people have the voice to influence their movies, rather than shutting down people and their ideas because of fear, control, ego, or insecurity.

Ever since I heard this producer's perspective, I've talked to a number of actors and directors in Hollywood who have helped me understand the real forces behind why bad movies and shows get made. It's almost never because of a shortage of good ideas or competent people.

Rather, it's because of the egos, insecure personalities, and processes that shut down the good ideas or never consult the competent people. There truly are empires of power and control in the movie industry that decide what and who to let in. Perhaps the same applies to many other organizations and industries.

When we talk about environments of oppression or freedom, it is true that we're talking about forces of power and control, right? Leaders are entrusted by an organization, a family, or a team with the power to make decisions that impact everyone. Their decisions — even in something seemingly minor like planning a meeting agenda — shape what kinds of topics will be discussed or not, and what kinds of voices will be heard and platformed, or not. Their degree of openness to input, feedback, and disagreement impacts how much others feel they can contribute.

As leaders, I often think we greatly underestimate our own power.

Feedback is a tool of power, because it involves forces of will and resistance. When we invite feedback, we hand others the stethoscope or microscope. **We ask them to enter into our space and speak into our lives.** It's an act of trust and vulnerability that requires inner strength and security.

When we invite feedback, we grant people the power to influence us.

When we shut down feedback, we use our power to resist, counter, or silence people and ideas. Either way, other leaders see and take note that "this is the way things are done here."

So what can we do, if we're stuck in an environment of oppression and control?

If we're the leader, or the person entrusted with most of the power:

A great first step is to (surprise!) start cultivating an environment where feedback and input is valued.

- **Start a regular feedback check-in time.**

At the end of each of your team meetings, allocate 10 minutes for a "feedback check-in" when everybody is asked to offer suggestions on what can be improved for the next meeting or give voice to topics that need more attention. I just talked to a leader who does this with his team, and it's been very effective for them.

If we're not the leader:

It's challenging but we can't settle for silence or victimhood.

- **Meet with the leader in person and share vulnerably and openly.**

  After the next team meeting, ask to meet up with the team leader individually and share with them your desire to be able to give more input and feedback to them and to the team. Ask specifically what can be done about this, and offer to help if desired or needed.

- **Model feedback yourself in front of the leader and team.**

  During a meeting, ask the other people on the team for feedback and input. Show them an experience of what it's like to be invited in and asked for help, and what it looks like to receive feedback well. It may catch on and become contagious! And if it doesn't, you can be a bit more direct and ask others to try requesting feedback on their projects.

  Or you can be more indirect and offer to implement a team process where every project goes through rounds of feedback, for the sake of greater productivity. Or you can suggest that your team watch a leadership training video on feedback and its applications, or even buy them a book about feedback!

There are a lot of ideas, but the point is that we can influence our environment, even when we're not the leader or don't have all the power. It may take time, but it can be done.

Questions for Small Groups & Coaches:

- Think about your family, work organization, and the main environments in your life. Which environment provides the most freedom, and which the least freedom? What you notice about how feedback is handled in these environments?

- *Action Step:* If you're leading a meeting, allocate the last ten minutes to get feedback on how things went and what could be improved.

- *Action Step:* If you're not leading a team or meeting, ask your leader individually if they would allocate some time for feedback. Or during the next meeting, ask your team, family, etc. for some feedback.

- *Action Step:* E-mail this booklet (*The Art of Growing Through Feedback*) to your team or family and invite them to go through it with you! Or e-mail a link to a video or buy them a book about feedback.

Chapter 9: Feedback and Ethnicity

Is there an "Asian American" way to handle feedback? How does ethnicity impact feedback processes and growth?

Ethnicity and differences matter. I've worked in ethnic and cross-cultural leadership development for the past decade, so everything I write comes from what I've learned in working with leaders from very different backgrounds and perspectives.

In my experience, there are two extremes when people start thinking about ethnic diversity and leadership:

1.   "People aren't that different."

This first mentality is that the most important principles of leadership *transcend* cultural differences. So for example, all the things I've discussed in my booklet on feedback should apply to anybody of any culture who reads it.

The problem when we take this mentality to an extreme is that we tend to make assumptions without asking, learning, and getting to know people who are different from us. It may be true that two people of different ethnicities are more similar than we think… but how will we truly know that unless we ask questions like, "What was it like for you growing up? What were things like in your family? How did you feel about being Latino?"

Even if some leadership principles are consistently true across cultures, there are always new insights and applications we can glean from people of diverse ethnic backgrounds and perspectives.

And we miss out in huge ways if we fail to see this.

2.   "You just don't understand, that doesn't work in my culture."

This second mentality is that leadership is quite different from one culture to another. So for example, someone might read my booklet on feedback and conclude, *"That's great, but does it really work for Asian Americans? Or for older generations? Is that just something for extroverts who like direct communication?"* And so on.

The problem when we take this mentality to an extreme is that we tend to "write things off" by stereotyping, which also inhibits learning and the leadership growth process. It may be true that there are components of feedback that are counter-intuitive or challenging to Asian Americans, but if that's the case shouldn't we explore what parts might apply and what parts might not? And why or why not?

Too often we use ethnic differences as a way to shut down the conversation or learning process, rather than move it forward.

So what can be done about this?

Let's try a "case study" of how we might evaluate this entire topic of feedback according to ethnicity:

1. **Majority culture case study: "People aren't that different"**

Let's say you're from the majority culture (Caucasian, if you live in the U.S.) and you lean towards Extreme Mentality #1 of "people aren't that different" when it comes to feedback. One thing you can do is simply find two people of different ethnicities than yourself and ask them:

- How did your family handle conflict growing up? How did your parents give you feedback? Did you ever feel the freedom to give them feedback?
- What is the hardest thing for you to do, when it comes to giving or receiving feedback? Why do you think it's so hard for you?

Then reflect with the other person:

- What was similar about our experiences and views on feedback?
- What was different about our experiences and views on feedback?
- What did you learn from the other person that you didn't know or understand before?

2.   Minority culture case study: "You just don't understand, that doesn't work in my culture"

Let's say you're from a minority culture (say Asian American, if you live in the U.S.) and you lean towards Extreme Mentality #2 of "you just don't understand, that doesn't work in my culture."

As a first step, think through the topic of feedback (for instance as outlined in my booklet) and then answer these questions:

- Which principles and ideas about feedback apply to Asian Americans, in your own experience?
- Which principles and ideas about feedback don't necessarily apply as well to Asian Americans, in your own experience? Why not?
- What principles or ideas would you suggest as an alternative to the ones listed, for Asian Americans?
- What applications would you suggest to better speak to Asian Americans?

Here's my take on how feedback plays out for a lot of Asian Americans. I say "a lot" because I don't like to overgeneralize, as there's a lot of diversity and variance even among Asian American cultures and generations.

A few of the cultural themes I see that impact the feedback process are:

1. The desire for harmony and avoidance of conflict (don't "rock the boat" or "make waves")
2. Quiet and indirectness in communication, out of deference and respect for others

3. Strong family structures and hierarchy, which make it harder to confront or critique authority

Again, I try not to go to Extreme Mentality # 1, which would be to just say, *"Get over it! You just have to be direct and confront people sometimes, even if it offends them."* I also try not to go to Extreme Mentality # 2, which would be to say, *"See! We just don't do feedback well, because of all these cultural factors."*

Instead, I see all these cultural themes as significant factors to pay attention to, because they influence and impact people. I see them as challenges that need creative solutions or approaches, so that our feedback process will be most effective and honoring to the people involved.

So for instance, maybe in some families I would need to bring up a feedback topic gently over the course of two meetings, rather than going "all out" with full blast intensity in the first meeting. Or maybe I'd need to show my respect by cooking dinner and sharing in a meal with my parents before bringing up a topic of feedback. Try to think about your family or context. What do you think would work for you? The key is to think creatively and constructively, instead of dismissing ideas or just getting stuck with no way to move forward.

As you look back on this booklet on feedback, you may notice that a lot of the wording and processes suggested are meant to be relational and honoring of people. I think a lot of them can work in your context, but sometimes we have to also think about the challenges we face and how to address them. That's part of the process of what it means to "contextualize" leadership for our setting... because there's no leadership material on any one topic that will speak perfectly to every culture, personality, generation, socio-economic class, and all of its nuances and challenges. We are the ones who get to do that through the process of exploring, trying, and learning!

May you find that process exciting, invigorating, and empowering!

Questions for Small Groups & Coaches:

- Which of the two "Extreme Mentalities" have you been exposed to more? What are your thoughts or concerns about these?

- *Action Step:* If you're from the majority culture, follow through on this case study.

- *Action Step:* If you're from a minority culture, follow through on this case study.

- Discuss how you've grown as you've gone through this (*The Art of Growing Through Feedback*) booklet. Where have you grown the most in confidence or skill? Where do you still need to grow? What's one thing about this process that's been unexpected or surprising for you?

- What's a practical way you can continue to interact with your group or coach, as you work on growing in feedback?

Appendix: What's Your Feedback Style?

One book I've found helpful about feedback is *Thanks For the Feedback* by **Douglas Stone and Sheila Heen.** It's practical, thoughtful, readable, and well-researched. I was inspired by a section in the book called "Feedback and You" that discusses the ways that we tend to react to feedback. The book lists five examples of different reactions, and it motivated me to come up with four categories of "feedback styles" (Two of these are similar to the book although I worded them quite differently, while the other two I wrote on my own):

1. I'm pretty sensitive to negative feedback, because of some bad experiences I've had over the years. I do want to hear and grow, but please be gentle with me!

2. Sometimes it takes me a while to digest and process feedback. So I'll tell you my first impressions, but please follow up with me tomorrow and I'll have even more to say.

3. Subtle feedback sometimes doesn't get through to me. Be respectful, but please be as explicit and direct as possible.

4. I'm not sure how I react to feedback, because I tend to associate it with doing occasional 360s and performance reviews. Please help me get more comfortable and grow in this area.

What I love about these categories is that the book talks about how when we understand our own style, it can actually make a huge difference in our ability to take in feedback. It says: "We're explaining our particular defensive formation not to block out the givers of feedback, but to help them get through to us." [6]

In other words, we're not using our feedback experiences or styles to *avoid* a conversation or justify why we don't want to hear feedback. This can happen easily... I might say, "I'm an internal processor, so I can't process and handle all of this right now!" or "I've had some bad experiences with feedback, so can you just give me some grace? Can we just forgive and

---

[6] Douglas Stone and Sheila Heen, *Thanks for the Feedback* (Penguin Books, 2015), 275.

forget?" And just like that, we've tried
to dodge feedback.

Instead, we can explain our feedback
styles to help people learn how to give us
feedback effectively and respectfully. We want to
let them in, not block them out.

If you're interested in exploring the topic of feedback
in more depth, I recommend *Thanks for the
Feedback*. It contains helpful charts and graphics
throughout, sample dialogues, and concise
summaries at the end of each chapter. Also, there's a
supplemental workbook called *Thank God for the
Feedback* that's designed for Christian leaders.

Let me know if you've found any other helpful
resources on feedback!

About Me

Hello, and thanks for reading this booklet! I'm a writer, speaker, and innovator who works in leadership development and ministry. My name (Adrian Pei) in Chinese means "honest scholar," and I try to live up to it. I live in southern California with my family. You can connect with me more at my website www.adrianpei.com or on Twitter @adrianpei.

Made in United States
Orlando, FL
14 May 2024

46864875R00046